40 Days to Your Best Life

FOR NURSES

HONOR HB BOOKS

Inspiration and Motivation for the Seasons of Life

COOK COMMUNICATIONS MINISTRIES
Colorado Springs, Colorado • Paris, Ontario
KINGSWAY COMMUNICATIONS LTD
Eastbourne, England

Honor® is an imprint of
Cook Communications Ministries, Colorado Springs, CO 80918
Cook Communications, Paris, Ontario
Kingsway Communications, Eastbourne, England

40 DAYS TO YOUR BEST LIFE FOR NURSES
© 2006 by Honor Books

Manuscript written by Suzanne Tietjen.
Interior Design: Sandy Flewelling (TrueBlue Design)
Cover Design: BMB Design

First Printing, 2006
Printed in the United States of America

2 3 4 5 6 7 8 9 10 Printing/Year 11 10 09 08 07 06

Author's Note: In order to protect the privacy of patients and their families, I have
changed names and any identifying details. The stories are otherwise true.

ISBN-13: 978-1-56292-706-6
ISBN-10: 1-56292-706-X

A Preface, of Sorts

Being a nurse is a privilege. Like many of my colleagues, I feel that it is also a calling.

But not the highest calling. That's reserved for God's call to believe and trust in his son.

Nurses *do* things.

Being a Christian is not about *doing* anything; it's about what's been done for us. It's not doing all the right things or even believing all the right things; it's about being in the right relationship—with Jesus Christ, Son of God, Savior.

He's the one who said, "Follow me."

These little stories are what happened when I did.

Day 1: Watered

WEARY AS I HAVE ever been, I waited for the cashier to call out my number. Italian takeout tonight. A night shift that ran too long and a nap that was way too short left me unwilling, if not unable, to cook dinner.

I was sagging on the bench, staring at nothing, when I heard a tiny voice say, "What do you do?"

A little girl, who looked to be maybe four years old, sat next to me. Her dad shushed her before I could answer. "Honey, let her be."

I smiled in spite of myself and said, "No, it's all right."

Then to her—"I'm a nurse. I take care of tiny babies."

Her eyes widened. "I'm gonna have a baby brother. We're getting dinner for Mommy because she's tired."

We talked about babies and how tired they can make their mommies. She told me she knew all that and she was going to be a helper.

Their number was called and they stood to collect their takeout packages and leave. But when they reached the door, the little girl softly touched her daddy's leg to stop him. She ran over to me with arms open, then hugged me tight.

"Take good care of the babies," she whispered, then turned and ran back to the door. Through the glass I watched her skip behind her dad to the car. My vision blurred.

God is present in our lives in so many ways. We may feel that we have given more than was wise. We're spent, empty, and struggling to go on.

God knows.

And he loves us.

He made sure I knew it that day.

Look for him in unexpected places. That's often where he is.

He who waters will himself be watered.

—Proverbs 11:25 NASB

Day 2: Too Posh to Wash?

"I DO NOT WASH people's bottoms. There are other people to do that."

So said one student nurse last year in Great Britain where new-generation nurses proposed that the caring element of their work be delegated to nursing assistants. The proposal was soundly defeated but provoked discussion as to why nurses do basic, and sometimes physically repelling, tasks.

The nurse who gives up those humble tasks surrenders time with the patient. Minutes spent bathing are not wasted—this is prime time to watch for signs of trouble that would be missed by a less-skilled assessor. Jeremy Bore, a prison nurse in Exeter said, "Nurses have been authorized to go where no other professional has been authorized to go—not even doctors, not even priests—and that is an enormous privilege."[1]

Human beings are messy things, even more so when we are ill. We eat and drink; then waste products come out. God made us this way and there is beauty in his design.

Most nurses get past the initial unpleasantness of dealing with the bathroom and bathing functions while they are still in nursing school. The best nurses can ease the feeling of shame and embarrassment experienced by an incontinent patient by treating the situation as a minor and everyday occurrence. We say, "Oh, don't worry about that! It's not a problem. We're used to taking care of things like that. Don't give it another thought," focusing on the patient's face while keeping a pleasant expression on our own.

Who, after all, is our model?

Jesus.

Jesus, who knelt to wash the feet of a ragtag group of fishermen.

He didn't think he was too good to do the dirty tasks.

Neither should we.

Your attitude should be the same that
Christ Jesus had. Though he was God,
he did not demand and cling to his rights as God.
He made himself nothing; he took the humble
position of a slave and appeared in human form.

—Philippians 2:5–7 NLT

Day 3: Getting In

BEING WELL OR GETTING sick really happens at the
level of the cell. The lay public sees only the external con-
sequences—physical symptoms such as nausea or
headache—without giving much thought to the microscopic
processes that are going on deep inside the body.

Medications have to get inside to help. Pills are swal-
lowed or placed under the tongue. Bronchodilators are
inhaled. Antibiotics are injected or infused. Pain medication
is gradually absorbed through the skin from a patch.
Nothing happens until the medication is inside and in the
right place to act.

The one who is sick has to acknowledge the illness and
take in the remedy. The patient has the right to refuse the
medicine; obviously, then, its benefit is lost.

Jesus said, "Healthy people don't need a doctor—sick

people do.… For I have come to call sinners, not those who think they are already good enough" (Matt. 9:12–13 NLT). Jesus recognized that a person who doesn't recognize (or want to admit) that he or she is sick won't seek help.

Many of us are unaware of our need for a Savior. We look around, compare ourselves with others, and think we're not so bad. Can God really mean it when he says that no one is righteous, not even one?

You bet.

No, we're not perfect. Who has never cheated, lied, gossiped, or hated? But God loved us enough to send his perfect son to pay for our sins. Our part is to realize our need and trust him.

If you have never done so before, ask him into your life now.

Don't refuse the cure.

Let him in.

**The mystery in a nutshell is just this:
Christ is in you, therefore you can look forward
to sharing in God's glory. It's that simple.**
—Colossians 1:27 MSG

Day 4: What Becomes of Our Failures?

SO MUCH OF WHAT we do comes to nothing. Or at least seems to.

We get up, shower, dress, and put on makeup or shave. Then we get into buses, trains, or cars and go where we need to go to do our work. We stuff our pockets with pens, scissors, a calculator. We scrub, get our assignments, and listen to reports. Then, only after all that, the work begins. Our patients' problems and needs fill the next eight (or more) hours of our lives.

We invest ourselves in taking care of others. We use our skills to put people in a place where healing can happen. Usually it works. Given rest, the right medications, and time, most people get well. Or at least better.

But sometimes they don't.

I've stood in the aftermath of a trauma, surrounded by

trash and blood, thinking, "What a waste. Did we accomplish anything?" We'd done our best, made every effort … and, in the end, failed.

Is anything gained?

The answer is yes, and it's more than just the judgment and experience we acquire.

One family made it clear to me when they came back with a meal to thank us. We tried to deflect their gratitude, still seeing our efforts as failure.

They weren't deterred. "We saw how hard you tried to save her. We could tell you loved her too." Through teary smiles and embraces, they comforted us as much as we comforted them.

No, our efforts are not wasted. There is beauty even in these failures. As Joyce Alexander, RN, MSN, said so well, "The rewards come from the same place as the pain."[2]

**It was a beautiful thing that you came
alongside me in my troubles.**
—Philippians 4:14 MSG

Day 5: The Secret of Brokenness

I take my heart in my hand,
O my God, O my God,
My broken heart in my hand:
Thou hast seen, judge thou.
—Christina Rossetti

MY ROTATION THROUGH PSYCH nursing was like entering an alternate universe. Patients who were psychotic were terrifying to me, with their inappropriate eye contact, delusional thinking, and lack of inhibition. Those less obviously ill scared me for another reason—they seemed too much like me. I'm so grateful for my instructor, a tiny East Indian woman with a gift for communicating with the mentally ill. She modeled active listening, formed connections through skilled use of body language, and defused potentially violent situations with a gently raised hand. Naïve and idealistic, we asked her how so many sick people could ever get well.

"They won't," she said. "Maybe with unlimited one-to-one counseling a good number of them could improve." She frowned. Staff and therapists were in short supply.

"So there's no hope." This from the class cynic.

I will never forget her answer.

"Only when each of these people comes to the end of himself—only then—will he have any chance to get well."

What is true for the mentally ill is also true for the spiritually sick. How often we try to pile up achievements—good works—to impress God. We try, and we fail; so we decide we must try harder. We ask God to help us, then, when we don't see him intervening, we step in and try to be the answer to our own prayer. What are we thinking?

We can't make an impression on God through our own efforts. God says all our righteous deeds are like a filthy garment (Isa. 64:6). Only when we realize our brokenness can God begin to work in and through us.

We, too, need to come to the end of ourselves. When we do, God will be right there.

The sacrifices of God are a broken spirit;
A broken and a contrite heart, O God,
You will not despise.
—Psalm 51:17 NASB

Day 6: Wee Worship

I WORK IN A Level III Neonatal Intensive Care Unit (NICU) with the sickest and tiniest of newborns. Smiles are rare on the faces of our patients. They undergo hundreds of painful experiences by the time they go home—if they go home. Some of them don't get that far.

It's especially difficult around the holidays. We pray that none of our little ones dies on Christmas. The grief would be compounded for years as the holiday turns into an anniversary of sorrow.

Two nurses in central Illinois have taken up the challenge of helping families living with the uncertainty of having a critically ill infant and families with the certainty of grief for a child who has died.

Jeanne Perino organizes a memorial service twice a year, at Easter and Christmas. Everyone is welcome. Music, poetry, and friendship ease the pain. Some families come once; some come every year.

Linda Koch makes sure that the little ones in the NICU have some Christmas memories. Each year, she recruits a staff member to dress up as Santa. The nurses dress the babies in their Christmas finery for a picture with the jolly elf. Santa holds the stronger ones or goes to the bedside for pictures with the weakest. Parents receive their baby's keepsake photograph in an envelope taped to the incubator.

This year one of our tiniest babies smiled for the camera.

The nurses laughed out loud when they saw the picture of his joyful expression smiling from the bulletin board in the break room. "You can almost hear him giggle, can't you?" one commented.

Nurses' smiles lingered when they walked from the break room into the unit. The joy of Christmas caught us by surprise where we least expected it.

A smile. A giggle. Joy. Worship.

God, brilliant Lord, yours is a household name.
Nursing infants gurgle choruses about you,
toddlers shout the songs that drown out enemy talk,
and silence atheist babble.
—Psalm 8:1–2 MSG

Day 7: The Incident Report

EVERY NURSE HAS FELT it—that sinking feeling when she realizes she has made a mistake. Sometimes—usually—she is the one to catch it. Then she wonders, at least for a moment, if she really needs to tell anyone. It's such a hassle. It will show up on her evaluation. The advantages of silence cross her mind.

It could be a calculation error, the wrong drug, or wrong patient. Sometimes the patient is harmed. Always there is the potential for harm.

Regardless, the nurse reaches for the incident report and sets it aside to fill out as soon as the patient's safety is assured. She notifies the nurse in charge and calls the doctor. After she takes action to prevent further problems, she will explain it all to the patient.

It's humbling.

And it's the right thing to do.

It hurts so much to be wrong. When a baker makes an error, he can throw out the cake. Nurses work in a profession where the stakes are high. Life and death. Permanent injury. Unnecessary suffering. The threat of a lawsuit.

It takes courage to finish the shift or come back the next day.

The Old Testament tells about cities of refuge, places where someone who had accidentally killed another could run to, places to be safe from those who demanded an eye for an eye, a life for a life. The refugee remained there, safe from vengeance, until the high priest died. Only then could the refugee return home.

We have a better refuge in Jesus. He says that his grace is sufficient and that his strength is made perfect in weakness. We can run to God with our failures, knowing that "Jesus, running on ahead of us, has taken up his permanent post as high priest for us" (Heb. 6:20 MSG). We are safe in him.

**The LORD is a shelter for the oppressed,
a refuge in times of trouble.**
—Psalm 9:9 NLT

Day 8: When You Walk In

WHEN HE WAS IN the fifth grade, my son Zack dislocated his neck while fooling around with friends in the swimming pool. He's grown now, but he recently shared with me again what his nurse meant to him during his hospitalization.

Zack's room was dark and he was all alone, his neck encased in a Phillips collar. He was scared, but every time his nurse came into his room, he felt safe. The nurse, a young African-American man, calmed Zack's fears about being paralyzed and explained how good it was that he felt the pain when the nurse pricked his toes.

Zack got tearful—he couldn't sit up or try to feed himself. His nurse was matter-of-fact, wiping Zack's tears with as much emotion as putting the spoon to Zack's lips. This nurse, by his manner, conveyed that tears were nothing to be ashamed of. This was important to a young boy who was trying hard to be brave.

"I don't even remember his name, but he was my guardian angel that night, settling me down when I couldn't move onto the gurney to go for my CAT scan," Zachary said. "When he was there, I knew I was okay."

So many times we think it is the high-tech procedures and the newest medications that are important to our work. In my son's case, it was the nurse's presence that made all the difference. That unnamed nurse was, himself, an instrument of healing. He watched my boy, realized his needs from moment to moment, and met them.

Zachary remembers listening for his footsteps.

Make a careful exploration of who you are and the work you have been given, and then sink yourself into that.... Each of you must take responsibility for doing the creative best you can with your own life.

—Galatians 6:4–5 MSG

Day 9: Silence Kills

THE SURGEON IS HERE to examine your patient, but he didn't wash his hands. Your friend contaminates the end of the IV tubing, then reaches to connect it to the patient.

What do you say? What do you do?

The American Association of Critical-Care Nurses and VitalSmarts Consulting Group recently publicized a study titled "Silence Kills."[3] Researchers found that 84 percent of doctors and 62 percent of nurses have seen colleagues making mistakes or otherwise engaging in unsafe care, but less than 10 percent of them approached their coworkers about their observations. Today's hospitals are working hard to promote a culture of safety, and they are beginning to recognize that this reluctance to confront—whether because of fear, sympathy, or timidity—is resulting in medical errors and substandard care.

The failure to confront is a serious problem for all of us. Jesus, though always loving, confronted others without fear. He said, "If you see your friend going wrong, correct him" (Luke 17:3 MSG). We can apply the principle of his instruction for dealing with our Christian brothers and sisters to our dealings with our coworkers. Jesus said, "If a fellow believer hurts you, go and tell him—work it out between the two of you. If he listens, you've made a friend. If he won't listen, take one or two others along … and try again. If he still won't listen, tell the church" (Matt. 18:15–17 MSG). In the health-care system, we can address lapses in care in the same step-by-step fashion.

But we can't remain silent.

Although those who found the courage to confront their coworkers were fewer than 10 percent, they affected the system positively, gaining better patient outcomes and higher job satisfaction.

We have an obligation to our patients and to the truth. Speak up.

Instead, we will lovingly follow the truth at all times—
speaking truly, dealing truly, living truly—
and so become more and more in every way like
Christ who is Head of his body, the church.

—Ephesians 4:15 TLB

Day 10: Pattern Recognition

A LOT OF WHAT we do as nurses involves pattern recognition. When a patient has one symptom, we note it, knowing that it could mean any number of things. When a second symptom joins the first, we think about it in the light of the first. We're narrowing the possibilities. If a third symptom occurs, we may recognize a pattern and form a provisional diagnosis in our mind. Our education and experience help us analyze the patterns we see. The more we practice, the better we can anticipate and often prevent further problems.

To do this, we need to be paying attention—watching, listening, observing. We need to know what's normal, so we can identify what isn't. We also need to be objective, thinking clearly and without prejudice.

Pattern recognition is a part of life. Jesus chided the

Pharisees for failing to recognize him as the Messiah after all their studying. They could predict the weather from the colors in the sky, but they couldn't see prophecy being fulfilled before their eyes. (See Matt. 16:2–3.)

We may be less skilled with pattern recognition in our personal lives. We may not have thought to apply these skills to this area. Self-examination, the counsel of a friend, or sharing with an accountability group may bring hidden symptoms to light.

Job prayed, "Make me to know my transgression and my sin" (Job 13:23 KJV). We, too, can ask God to reveal tendencies and patterns in our lives that don't please him. God is full of mercy. He will make us aware of our sin as soon as we ask him.

An early diagnosis yields the best prognosis.

**Thus says the LORD of hosts:
"Consider your ways!"**
—Haggai 1:7 NKJV

Day 11: Seeing Jesus

CLINIC PATIENTS. FREQUENT FLIERS in the ER. Who are they really?

If we're to believe Mother Teresa, who gave her life to caring for the poor and dying in India, they are Jesus in one of his many "distressing disguises." She said that if our lives are centered on Jesus' body and blood, it will be easy to see "Christ in that hungry one next door, the one lying in the gutter, that alcoholic man we shun, our husband, our wife, or our restless child."[4]

It might have been easy for her.

It's an ongoing struggle for me.

I find myself being judgmental, even cracking jokes about these less fortunate ones.

May God forgive me.

May he forgive us all.

Jesus told a story about those who would inherit his kingdom. He said, "I was hungry, and you gave Me something to eat; I was thirsty, and you gave Me something to drink; I was a stranger, and you invited Me in; naked, and you clothed me; I was sick, and you visited Me; I was in prison, and you came to Me" (Matt. 25:35–36 NASB).

The righteous asked him, When? When did they do these things?

His answer? "When you did it to one of the least of these My brethren, you did it to Me" (Matt. 25:40 NKJV).

A sobering thought for Jesus' audience.

And for me.

Like Mother Teresa, my heart's desire is to know Jesus. I'll find him where she found him—in the faces of the suffering.

Real religion, the kind that passes muster
before God the Father, is this:
Reach out to the homeless
and loveless in their plight.
—James 1:27 MSG

Day 12: Most Trusted

IN 2004, FOR THE fifth time in six years, nurses came first in the Gallup survey of the most trusted professions.[5] We are rated higher than teachers, doctors, clergy, and judges. Despite stereotyped and inaccurate portrayals of nurses in the media, the public finds us trustworthy.

Is it because of the stories we read in elementary school about Clara Barton, the angel of the battlefield? Is it because everyone knows we aren't in this profession for the money? Or is it because most people have needed a nurse at a low point in their lives and encountered one who saw them as they were, met needs they weren't even aware of, and anchored them in the storm?

To know that so many people trust us is heartwarming. It's good—and necessary—to be trusted. Without our patients' trust, we find it difficult if not impossible to help them.

Years ago, I cared for a man with a pneumonia that was resistant to every available antibiotic. The Centers for Disease Control got involved, taking samples of the bacteria that threatened his life. We could only offer supportive care, which he resisted. I remember trying to encourage him to drink more water. He refused. Whatever we proposed, he rejected. I longed for his trust, but was unable to help him.

God, too, longs for our trust. He promises peace, joy, safety, mercy—every possible blessing to those who will trust him. In verse after verse of his Word, he asks for our trust. But he doesn't force himself on anyone. Just as I was limited in the care I could offer my reluctant patient, God will not impose his blessings on someone who rejects him.

God is first on the list of the trustworthy.

We who are trusted can trust him.

Taste and see that the LORD is good. Oh, the joys of those who trust in him!
—Psalm 34:8 NLT

Day 13: Not on My Shift

RECENTLY A FRIEND RECOUNTED a conversation she'd had with a patient.

"This man told me he thought today was the day he was going to die. We'd gotten to know each other pretty well, so I felt sure enough of his sense of humor to say what I was really thinking: 'Not on my shift, you don't!'"

"You didn't! What did he say?"

"He laughed with me. I joked with him about how much paperwork that would generate."

She took a sip of her coffee and shook her head slowly. "I guess he didn't want to cause any trouble, because he didn't die."

Not on my shift. We've all thought it, even if we've never come right out and said it. We don't want our patients to die on us. And of course it's not because of the paperwork.

Death is the enemy.

We want to save lives. To make it all better.

Death we avoid—when we can. All nurses cope with death in our work. Getting used to it is not the same as coming to terms with it. We need to work through our own issues before we can deal holistically with life's end.

The Bible says "the very last enemy is death" (1 Cor. 15:26 MSG). We'll see the end of dying when God's kingdom is come. Until then, everyone will face death.

But God saves those who believe on his son. By his death, he overcame death. And he promises to wipe away all tears. (See Rev. 21:4.)

We probably can't help praying "Not on my shift," but we can always take comfort in God's saving grace.

**Precious in the sight of the LORD
is the death of his saints.**
—Psalm 116:15 KJV

Day 14: The Promise

I WAS A NEOPHYTE and not one to question the rules. Death was new to me when I spent my shift helping a mother and father work through fresh grief for their baby. Crying, they bathed Braden, then dressed him in what should have been his going-home outfit. At one point, Braden's daddy removed a thick gold chain from his own neck and placed it around the baby's. When they were ready to leave, I began to remove the necklace so they could take it with them. I explained that the hospital had a policy of never leaving valuables with the deceased because we couldn't guarantee their safety.

Tears welled up in the father's eyes. "Don't you take that off. I put it on him and it's never coming off."

I wasn't sure what to do. I wanted to honor the family's wishes, but I didn't want the necklace stolen or lost. I have to admit, too, that I was afraid to break the rules.

"Give me a minute. Let me think," I said. Then I prayed silently. *What do I do?*

I called the supervisor, who reinforced hospital policy. In that moment, God gave me the courage to be an advocate for this family. I told the supervisor the story, then asked her if there was any way to follow the family's wishes. I suggested securing the chain with adhesive tape so that it could not slip off, documenting this in the chart, and calling the funeral home to inform them that the family wanted the chain to stay on Braden even for burial. To my surprise she agreed with this plan, and so did the family and funeral home. Braden wore the chain to his grave, a symbol of his father's love.

And I learned that rules, though necessary, are not always written in stone.

Love is greater than the law.

The entire law is summed up in a single command:
"Love your neighbor as yourself."
—Galatians 5:14

Day 15: Noncompliance

HE'S BACK IN THE ER again, his chart flagged "NC" for noncompliant. His blood sugar is soaring and his glucose monitoring device tells the story. The data is there—how often he checks his sugar, along with a set of results that show that he isn't in good control. As his nurse, you'll start all over again, educating, demonstrating, and answering questions. You know he can't be following his diet. His explanations don't ring true. In times like these, you may feel like you're wasting your breath on people who don't cooperate in their own care.

Noncompliance takes many forms: a pregnant teen with frequent no-shows at the prenatal clinic, an alcoholic losing the struggle with addiction, even an elderly grandmother cutting her pills in half to save money. All of them are court-ing disaster by not complying with their health-care plan.

Hard not to be judgmental, isn't it?

Think about how God feels.

Isaiah, the prophet says, "Woe to those who go to great depths to hide their plans from the LORD, who do their work in darkness and think, 'Who sees us? Who will know?' You turn things upside down, as if the potter were thought to be like the clay! Shall what is formed say to him who formed it, 'He did not make me'? Can the pot say of the potter, 'He knows nothing'?" (Isa. 29:15–16).

Talk about noncompliance.

God wants us to be yielded and trusting him in his plan for our lives. So often we are not.

Help us, God, to give up, to surrender. Like clay, may we be soft and pliable in your hands, trusting that your ways are best.

Yet, O LORD, you are our Father.
We are the clay, you are the potter;
we are all the work of your hand.
—Isaiah 64:8

Day 16: What's Inside

IMPATIENCE IS MY BESETTING sin. Many nurses struggle with it. How we handle frustration says a lot about who we are as Christians.

The world has changed. Patients are sicker and they live longer—long enough to acquire multiple diseases with complex therapies.

The hurry-up pace combined with a slow computer or a missing medication can raise my frustration level to overload. When the irritations reach critical mass, my voice can take on a sharp edge and, before I know it, I've said or done something to make the situation worse.

I used to think that circumstances were causing my impatience and frustration. As it turns out, that's not the case. Jesus taught his followers that circumstances don't make a person different; rather, they reveal the person for who she really is.

If you knock over a cup of antacid on the med tray, what spills out of it? That's right—the chalky, white antacid. The only thing that can spill out of a container is the substance it contains.

So if my day is going badly, I may succeed in hiding my frustration for a while. But eventually someone will bump me. When that happens, whatever is inside me will overflow. If I'm trusting God with my day and counting it all joy, then joy will pour out on that person who came up against me. If I'm carrying my load alone, feeling like it all depends on me, allowing the pressure to build and build, then when someone bumps into me—that person's really going to get it.

The solution? "Put yourself aside, and help others get ahead. Don't be obsessed with getting your own advantage. Forget yourselves long enough to lend a helping hand. Think of yourselves the way Christ Jesus thought of himself" (Phil. 2:3–5 MSG).

Countercultural, isn't it?

Sure.

What's in you?

Be filled instead with the Holy Spirit,
and controlled by him.
—Ephesians 5:18 TLB

Day 17: Making a Dent

I ALWAYS KNOW IT'S bad when I hit the back hall and see a couple of transporters waiting to be cleaned and people ducking in and out of rooms like in one of those crazy Marx Brothers movies. Or when I'm walking through the parking lot and a departing coworker says, "Run—run like the wind!" then laughs because she's leaving and I can't.

I console myself. *It'll pass. Nothing lasts forever.*

But I know I'll pay a price, incur some damage.

I pray I'll make a dent, do some good, make a difference. I hang onto this hope.

Like a grain of sand on the beach, we are lost in the enormity of the work we do. Positive feedback can be rare and negativity all too frequent.

Why do we do what we do?

Because of the need.

The work calls to us, whispers our name. It shouts and pleads for our help like a beggar. We don't—we can't—walk by.

We have something to offer, so we offer it. We take a deep breath and enter the fray, starting an IV here, setting up a procedure tray there—maybe just handing a tissue to wipe a tear. We know we can't "make it all better," but we can surely make one thing better.

And then another.

Whatever our hands find to do, we can do with all our might (Eccl. 9:10, paraphrased). God can do a lot with our little.

And when we offer our work to other people on behalf of God, we can ask him to bless it. Even if we never see the results, he will make more of it than we can imagine.

Offer it up.

**Let the loveliness of our Lord, our God,
rest on us, confirming the work that we do.
Oh, yes. Affirm the work that we do.**
—Psalm 90:17 MSG

Day 18: It's in the Blood

For the life of any creature is in its blood.
—Leviticus 17:11 NLT

THE PATIENT SWAYS THE first time you assist him to dangle his legs over the edge of the bed.

"Tell me what's happening." You help him to lie flat; then reach for his pulse, which is swift and thready.

"Just a little lightheaded," he says.

You check his dressing. Dry. Once you're sure he isn't in immediate danger, you call the doctor for orders. A few hours later your patient is much improved after receiving a transfusion.

Downstairs in the ER, trauma nurses recycle blood from a hemothorax back to the patient so he won't bleed out.

Every nurse knows that life is in the blood. A 10 percent loss puts the patient into shock, the slippery slope toward death. A 25 to 30 percent loss can be fatal. In a very real sense, lack of blood flow is a part of every death.

Our spiritual lives depend on blood as well—the blood of Jesus. Not only did his death put believers into a right relationship with God, his sacrifice goes on cleansing us from the wrong things we do. Just as the cells of our body depend on the flow of blood to bring oxygen and nutrients and take away waste products, we depend on God from moment to moment to guide us and to pardon our shortcomings (some people might call them sins—and they'd be right).

Peroxide takes a blood stain out of your uniform. The blood of Jesus works like that when we admit we're wrong and ask forgiveness.

It costs us nothing.

It cost him everything.

But if we [really] are living and walking
in the Light, as He [Himself] is in the Light,
we have [true, unbroken] fellowship
with one another, and the blood of Jesus Christ
His Son cleanses (removes) us from all
sin and guilt [keeps us cleansed from sin
in all its forms and manifestations].

—1 John 1:7 AB

Day 19: He Gives His Beloved Sleep

THREE A.M. FEELING a little chilled, you reach for your scrub jacket. Your body temperature is at its lowest ebb.

Will this night ever end?

Nurses understand like few others the longing for morning. It's a small club—nurses, residents, police officers, firefighters—they work while most people sleep. A $2 shift differential in pay probably doesn't compensate for the true cost of shift work.

Researchers have discovered higher rates of certain cancers and other diseases in those who work the late shift. Life expectancy is lower by seven to eight years. Besides physical disease, the risk of accident is higher. Most nurses know at least one horror story of a friend falling asleep at the wheel. Many night-shift nurses report arriving home without remembering the trip.

As if the risks to our own well-being aren't enough, the safety of those we care for is also compromised through lack of sleep. Our three a.m. critical thinking and physical dexterity are as impaired as someone with a 0.05 percent blood alcohol level. After 24 hours awake, our performance is comparable to that of the legally drunk—a 1.0 percent blood alcohol level.[6] Just as with alcohol, the individual coping with fatigue is not a good judge of the level of impairment. Nurses who would never work under the influence of alcohol or medications show up to work without a good day's rest or even a nap. And hospital rules often prohibit sleeping, even on breaks.

God, who made us, understands. David wrote:

> *My life's on the line before God, my Lord,*
> *waiting and watching till morning,*
> *waiting and watching till morning.*
>
> —*Psalm 130:6* MSG

How do we respond to the problem? Sleep. Take care of the needs of our bodies. Talk to administrators about the benefits of brief naps during breaks.

Again, and most importantly, sleep.

It is senseless for you to work
so hard from early morning until late at night,
fearing you will starve to death; for God
wants his loved ones to get their proper rest.

—Psalm 127:2 TLB

Day 20: My Prayer—
and Its Difficult Answer

The clouds are known to gather
and the wind is prone to blow
I'll keep her steady as a river
When the wild wind comes to blow
I've already been delivered
So I'll keep her steady as she goes.[7]
—Andrew Peterson

I TAPPED MY FINGERS on the steering wheel to these lyrics as I prayed, "Let me set my course for what you want tonight. Teach me to trust you."

The track advanced, and as quickly as that my commitment flagged. I wasn't sure I felt strong enough for the kind of lessons God teaches me in the Neonatal Intensive Care Unit. "Uh, God? Could you maybe use some experience I've already had rather than a new one?" I had a feeling of dread about the upcoming shift, and I regretted my prayer. Did that mean I didn't trust him?

Well, yes, I guess it did.

An hour into the shift I admitted an extremely low-birth-weight infant whose circulation failed to make the transition to life outside the womb. Our team exhausted every option during the next eight hours but still lost the battle.

His exhausted mother said, "I know God has a purpose for his life."

I'm sure of it. But who can say what that purpose was?

We shed tears together, full of questions.

Each of us had lent our skills to the task. We wanted to save a life, but we failed. Now we used other skills to hold up the grieving family as they held their dying child. In the aftermath, I watched as nurses, physicians, respiratory therapists, clerks, and technicians hugged and affirmed each other in our smaller sorrow.

The family got through it. And so did we.

And what of my prayer? God answered it.

When knowledge and expertise fail, trust is all we have left. We can't will an outcome. All outcomes are in his hands.

And in the sorrow, we were bathed in his love.

That, we got right.

**You're blessed when you stay on course,
walking steadily on the road revealed by God.**

—Psalm 119:1 MSG

Day 21: Jesus in Us

Jesus is completely and utterly sufficient.
Yet, he has chosen to be seen through the lens of our lives.[8]
—Fawn Parish

SOMETIMES PARENTS IN OUR Neonatal Intensive Care Unit get caught up in the action that is taking place around them. They watch, enthralled, as if they were in the middle of a TV drama. We gently try to help them to focus on their baby, who needs their presence.

Knowing where to look can be a problem for Christians, as well.

Living our faith can be a paradox. On one hand, what we do matters—people who would never read a Bible or visit a church are watching us and observing how we act toward others. Through our actions, we show them what God is like.

On the other hand, we don't matter at all. The apostle Paul said, "The life you see me living is not 'mine,' but it is lived by faith in the Son of God, who loved me and gave himself for me" (Gal. 2:20 MSG).

Our motivation is the key. Our attention must be firmly on God, as we live in joyful obedience. It's okay to be peripherally aware that others are watching. After all, Jesus said, "Let your light so shine before men, that they may see your good works, and glorify your Father which is in heaven" (Matt. 5:16 KJV). But we need to careful not to do good things so people will be impressed with us.

Like a lens, we must be focused on the object of our faith. We look at our Lord, and an amazing thing happens. "We Christians … can be mirrors that brightly reflect the glory of the Lord. And as the Spirit of the Lord works within us, we become more and more like him" (2 Cor. 3:18 TLB).

People will see Jesus in us.

Wow.

Keep your eyes on Jesus.

—Hebrews 12:2 TLB

Day 22: Holding Still

MY FRIENDS IN THE ER used to say, "We love a crying kid."

It was true. If the kids were well enough to yell and cry, we knew we had something to work with. The silent ones, lying motionless—they were the ones who scared us.

Still, the struggling screamers presented us with a problem. They didn't hold still—so we couldn't take care of them. After battling through the exam, we reached for the "papoose," a blue cotton-duck restraint device that snugly wrapped the child so we could do what needed to be done.

I, too, have a hard time holding still. Like most nurses, I am quick to act, seeing needs and moving to meet them. Unfortunately, the needs are infinite. And I am not. I wear myself out trying to fix things, and I stop only when I'm too tired to go on.

This makes it hard for God to work on me. He invites me to be still and know him. I am amazed at how many times God asked his people to be still, to stand still. When they did, God revealed himself.

Isaiah told Israel God's solemn counsel: "Your salvation requires you to turn back to me and stop your silly efforts to save yourselves. Your strength will come from settling down in complete dependence on me—The very thing you've been unwilling to do. You've said, 'Nothing doing! We'll rush off on horseback! ... We'll ride off on fast horses!' ... Think again: ... God takes the time to do everything right—everything. Those who wait around for him are the lucky ones" (Isa. 30:15–18 MSG).

I'm grateful that God keeps reminding me to stop, be still, and listen to him. I can't hear his still, small voice in the rushing.

In quietness and confidence shall be your strength.
—Isaiah 30:15 NKJV

Day 23: Going On?

MOST NURSES HAVE BEEN asked the question. You know the one—"You're so smart. Why don't you go on to be a doctor?"

The questioners don't mean to offend. But their premise is all wrong. Being a nurse is not a step in a progression that leads to the higher position of doctor. Nursing is not the same as medicine. At the risk of oversimplifying, medicine is focused on the disease process, while nursing is focused on support—placing the patient in the best position for healing to take place.

Still, the public sees physicians as more valuable, on the whole, than nurses. Maybe it's because they earn more money; maybe it's because doctors write orders and nurses carry them out. We are aware of this lower status, this lack of respect, as we carry out our work each day.

"I know I'm just the nurse" is an all-too-frequent preface to our observations, and by using it, we devalue those observations. Our perspective, our voice, is important to a holistic view of the patient. If we "go on" to become doctors or belittle what we alone can offer, everyone loses.

God doesn't see things the same way we do. Human status, positions in society—these mean nothing to God. There is no partiality with him. (See Eph. 6:9.) What matters to God is that we do well what he has given us to do. God, who is no respecter of persons, says, "Whatever you do, do your work heartily, as for the Lord rather than for men" (Col. 3:23 NASB).

Nurses aren't "just" anything. Our work has real and lasting significance. We don't need to define ourselves in anyone's eyes but God's.

Let every detail in your lives—words, actions,
whatever—be done in the name of the Master, Jesus,
thanking God the Father every step of the way.
—Colossians 3:17 MSG

Day 24: How He Loves

HUMAN LOVE IS FLAWED. Battered women, abused children, broken vows. We start out to love. We mean to do it. But something goes wrong. Even in the most successful marriages and the strongest friendships, love fails sometimes.

Love is there, to be sure. The bruised toddler wails at being taken from the parent who caused him harm. The injury is compounded by the loss of love. People we love will disappoint us. And we will disappoint them as well. When you've been hurt by someone you love, trust comes hard, if at all.

We try to understand God in the light of our own experiences, and this creates a problem. We are afraid that God's love is like ours.

It is not.

I talked with a pediatric intensive care nurse recently who said, "It's a wonder any of us who work here believe in God; much less that he is good." Yet she does believe. She takes it on faith that God loves us and that his love is different from any love we've experienced. The Bible says that God is love (see 1 John 4:8) and goes on to describe that love as selfless, humble, endless, and always looking for the best. (See 1 Cor. 13.)

So how do we love like God? If we rely on ourselves, it's impossible.

Instead, we watch God and learn from him. The Bible says that "mostly what God does is love you. Keep company with him and learn a life of love. Observe how Christ loved us. His love was not cautious but extravagant. He didn't love in order to get something from us but to give everything of himself to us. Love like that" (Eph. 5:2 MSG).

He wouldn't ask us to do it if he couldn't make us able.

Love like that.

**Go after a life of love as if your life
depended on it—because it does.**
—1 Corinthians 14:1 MSG

Day 25: Focus

IN 1999, THE INSTITUTE of Medicine issued a report titled "To Err is Human," saying that one in twenty-five hospital patients is harmed by medical errors.[9] Medical errors are the eighth highest cause of death in the United States, outranking automobile accidents, breast cancer, and HIV/AIDS. My father, an aerospace engineer—and thus a person with a low tolerance for errors—couldn't get over this.

"How can this happen?" he asked me.

I told him to imagine himself sitting at the dinner table reaching for the salt when Mom asks him a question. A moment later he finds himself shaking pepper rather than salt onto his mashed potatoes. It happens just like that.

Distraction, it turns out, is the root cause of errors about 41 percent of the time.[10] The health-care world is struggling to find ways to avoid interruptions and concentrate on the task at hand.

Distraction gets me in trouble spiritually as well. I battle it daily in my prayer life. I start out talking to God and somehow find myself making a grocery list. Or I plan to read my Bible, but get caught up in a television show.

Worse still, I have an impulse to call a friend or write a letter, but between the demands of work and home, I forget to do it. I find myself reacting to life's interruptions, rather than following God's leading. All too human, I can't maintain my focus on my own.

The apostle Paul talked about having his eye on the goal. More and more—at work, at home, and in my relationships with God and people—I, too, am asking God to help me pay attention.

One thing at a time.

Focus on the goal.

Eyes on the prize.

His life in me.

The way to life—to God!—is vigorous
and requires your total attention.

—Luke 13:24 MSG

Day 26: His Word in the Palm of My Hand

Thy word is a lamp unto my feet,
and a light unto my path.
—Psalm 119:105 KJV

IT'S A HURRY-UP WORLD we live in. When I don't set the alarm early enough, I race to work without reading my Bible at the start of my day. Then I'm exhausted after work and fall asleep without getting in the Word at day's end. There are always breaks. I take that back—we nurses know that we often forfeit our breaks. When we do get a few minutes, we're not likely to have a Bible in our hands.

A personal digital assistant (PDA) can change all that. Combination calculator, calendar, and medication book, a

PDA can also hold an electronic Bible. I bought one online, but Christian bookstores sell them too. Mine has changed my life.

When I need encouragement, I'm a click away from David's psalms. I've searched for an elusive verse, highlighted favorites, and grown in my relationship to God.

It's all right there. Every benefit God promises—protection, wisdom, discernment, comfort.

I can open this Bible wherever I am. And God can use it to equip me to serve him. God's Word "is useful to teach us what is true and to make us realize what is wrong in our lives. It straightens us out and teaches us to do what is right" (2 Tim. 3:16 NLT).

If you don't have a PDA, don't worry. A tiny New Testament will fit right in your pocket next to the scissors.

Now you're ready for anything.

**Through the Word we are put together and shaped
up for the tasks God has for us.**

−2 Timothy 3:17 MSG

Day 27: The Most Important Moment

THE RINGING PHONE CUT into my relaxed, day-off mode. Thirty minutes later I found myself in an ambulance, speeding north to transport a very sick newborn. The tiny girl needed the most extreme therapy we offer—Extra-Corporeal Membrane Oxygenation (ECMO). We were traveling with nitric oxide on board to help blood flow to her lungs. Unfortunately, she was sicker than we had been told. We started the nitric oxide on the elevator as we scrambled to get to the ECMO machine before she died. Just as we were ready to pull out of the ambulance bay, her mother arrived in a wheelchair, accompanied by her out-of-breath father. They wanted a chance to see her and touch her one last time before she left. I hesitated—she was so unstable—then nodded and helped her mom onto the rig.

They weren't there very long but it felt like forever. I

caught myself tapping my foot, then stopped and prayed instead. When we drove away, I saw the mother's hand flapping a weak good-bye.

It was all we could do to keep her alive during the trip. We jogged down the hall and into the ICU with her heart still beating. Then, as we placed her under the warmer, her heart stopped. She was gone and nothing the team tried brought her back.

That experience forever changed the way I think about what's important. I thought I was there to save that child's life. Speed was crucial; superior technology was paramount.

I was wrong.

I didn't—couldn't—know the end of the story. All the things I thought were so important made no difference in the end.

The most important thing we did that day? Giving those parents the time they needed with their baby. Time to relate. To love.

God knew. May we always be sensitive to his leading.

Give me insight so I can do what you tell me—my whole life one long, obedient response.

—Psalm 119:34 MSG

Day 28: Eating Our Young?

Be ye kind one to another.
—Ephesians 4:32 KJV

THE DAY'S SHAPING UP to be a busy one. It'll be all you can do to keep up. Then you see who's got the other end of the floor.

The new graduate. Not an orientee—that wouldn't be so bad; she would be the preceptor's responsibility. And another strong back for lifting help if nothing else. No, you're assigned with a new nurse, one who's finished orientation.

On a day you need help, you'll be required to give it.

Most of us feel a twinge of guilt at thoughts like these. We may never admit them to anyone else. But we have them.

We tell ourselves that we were new once too. We remind ourselves of nurses who were kind to us when we were inexperienced. We force a smile and try to be kind.

Often we fail. The nature of our work—stress, frustration, whatever—leads to failure. We end up criticizing, complaining, or gossiping about our less-experienced coworker. Nurses are notorious for eating our young.

Yes, we feel bad about it, but how do we stop it?

Not by trying harder. But by realizing we can't.

If we could "be good" just by trying harder, we wouldn't have needed a Savior.

Instead, do what the Bible says and change your mindset. Colossians 3 says to consider ourselves dead to the wrong things we do and put them aside, then put on a new self who is being changed to be like Jesus. God says "put on a heart of compassion, kindness, humility, gentleness and patience" (v. 12 NASB). We can trust God to provide the feelings to go with the actions he wants.

Start with a word of praise or kindness.

Go on.

Say it.

She'll never forget how you made her feel.

**Anxiety in a man's heart weighs it down,
but a good word makes it glad.**
—Proverbs 12:25 NASB

Day 29: Fall Prevention

MY HOSPITAL HAS AN initiative to prevent patient falls. Maybe yours does too. Patients are assessed upon admission, after procedures, or post-sedation for their risk of falling. Those most vulnerable wear green armbands, and their doors bear green signs to alert the staff. Fall status is communicated at every shift change during their stay. Caregivers take care to place items within easy reach and arrange the environment for safety, even to the point of providing special slippers for extra traction. We take falling very seriously and hope that by these measures we can prevent many falls.

God, too, takes falling very seriously. Long before there were hospitals, he had his own fall prevention program outlined in the Bible. Solomon, the wisest man who ever lived, tells us the risk factors: trusting in your riches or material things (see Prov. 11:28), plotting against others (see Prov. 26:27), hardening your heart (see Prov. 28:14), willfully doing wrong (see Prov. 28:18), and being arrogant (see Prov. 16:18). All of these actions and attitudes set us up for a fall.

I know I have exhibited every one of them.

Assess your risk.

Next, take action. Solomon says that accepting instruction (see Prov. 10:8), hearing wise counsel (see Prov. 11:14), and maintaining healthy friendships (see Eccl. 4:10) will prevent falls. Peter exhorted the early Christians to grow in their faith to prevent stumbling. (See 2 Peter 1:1–10.)

Hospitals can't prevent every fall, and neither can we. Give thanks that "the steps of a man are established by the LORD, and He delights in his way. When he falls, he will not be hurled headlong, because the LORD is the One who holds his hand" (Ps. 37:23–24 NASB).

Hang onto his hand, get back up, and walk on.

He has told you, O man, what is good;
And what does the LORD require of you
But to do justice, to love kindness,
And to walk humbly with your God?
—Micah 6:8 NASB

Day 30: Compassion Fatigue

NURSES CARE. IT'S WHAT we do. So what kind of a crisis is it when we find that we don't care?

Or maybe can't care?

Most people deal with suffering and death infrequently. Conversely, it is the daily bread of nurses. We hear the horror stories—see them and feel them. But the shift isn't over. Our patients still need us. So we soldier on.

To cope, we concentrate on the task instead of the person until the worst of it is over. Then one day we hear a patient's story that we know should touch us—but it doesn't. We are emotionally exhausted, caught in the grip of compassion fatigue.

I've beaten myself up over this. Sometimes my heart is cold and dead inside my chest. Then I feel guilty because I can't muster up any emotion.

I decide I am a bad person—a terrible nurse.

It drives me to my knees.

That turns out to be a good thing, because God is compassionate. My love is a weak thing, prone to failure; God's love is different in its very essence. Five times the Psalms describe God as being full of compassion. Over and over he showed compassion to his wayward children, Israel.

Jesus was moved by compassion, especially in his healing ministry. Yet he said, "The Son can do nothing by himself. He does only what he sees the Father doing" (John 5:19 NLT). Jesus, too, got tired. We don't know if he experienced compassion fatigue, but we do know that he regularly withdrew from the crowds and talked with his Father. We can follow his example, forming fleeting silent prayers as we work, then withdrawing when circumstances allow.

God is the source of the love we share with others.

Draw deeply from that source.

Keep yourselves in the love of God, looking for the
mercy of our Lord Jesus Christ unto eternal life.
And of some have compassion, making a difference.
—Jude 21–22 KJV

Day 31: Celebrate

Celebrate God all day, every day. I mean, revel in him!
—Philippians 4:4 MSG

ONE OF THE NICEST things about my unit is our habit of celebrating. We light candles on birthday cakes and hang crepe paper for wedding and baby showers. Weekend potlucks feed body and soul. Sales representatives have used themes and refreshments to relate to our staff. We even have a spirit committee that helps us develop our sense of play.

We enjoy celebration. It lifts our spirits and binds us together.

Should we be surprised to find that God, too, likes celebration? King David danced before God with all his might, embarrassing his wife, but pleasing God. The Old Testament is full of celebrations (they called them feasts) that spoke deeply to the hearts of the Israelites about their God.

The book of Nehemiah reports that the Israelites rebuilt the walls of Jerusalem then listened as Ezra, the prophet, read God's Word. They responded in worship and with weeping. Nehemiah, Ezra, and the priests told them not to cry but to celebrate, preparing feasts and sharing with those who had nothing because "the joy of the LORD is your strength" (Neh. 8:10). *The Message* version reads, "So the people went off to feast, eating and drinking and including the poor in a great celebration. Now they got it; they understood the reading that had been given to them" (Neh. 8:12).

Like the weeping Israelites, I tend to beat myself up when I'm wrong. Repentance is necessary, but God doesn't intend us to remain in that place, centered on ourselves, wallowing in our misery. He wants us to accept his love and then to party, always including those who have nothing. Joy is an endpoint in this walk.

So celebrate.

Thou shalt rejoice before the L<small>ORD</small> thy God in all that thou puttest thine hands unto.

—Deuteronomy 12:18 KJV

Day 32: Changed

MATTER IS NEITHER CREATED nor destroyed. The food we eat breaks down into smaller parts: fatty acids, proteins, and other microscopic bits. Then they're changed into other things: muscles, bone, nerves, and cartilage. The liquids we drink are mostly water. The water molecules from these liquids travel through the system "morphing" into other things: spinal fluid, urine, lymph, tears—even the vitreous humor in our eyes.

What we take in becomes us. Substances travel to different locations—heart, brain, or pinky finger—and stay anywhere from a few hours to the rest of our lives. Most of us remember enough from our nutrition courses in nursing school to know how to eat a healthy diet—even if we don't always do it.

We may not be quite as careful about what we take into

our minds through our eyes and ears. Many Christians, male and female, struggle with pornography. All of us decide what books to read and which television shows to watch. Striking images actually hardwire nerve connections in our brains—almost like burning a DVD. We are altered by every experience.

God, who loves us more than we can imagine, tells us that "you'll do best by filling your minds and meditating on things true, noble, reputable, authentic, compelling, gracious—the best, not the worst; the beautiful, not the ugly; things to praise, not things to curse" (Phil. 4:8 MSG).

We become what we take in.

May God himself, the God who makes everything
holy and whole, make you holy and whole,
put you together—spirit, soul, and body—and keep
you fit for the coming of our Master, Jesus Christ.

1 Thessalonians 5:23 MSG

Day 33: An Unguarded Heart

MORNING ROUNDS IN THE Neonatal Intensive Care Unit. We sat in the center of the room discussing each small patient and planning every aspect of their next twenty-four hours. The neonatologist's cell phone interrupted our work and, as it looked as though the conversation would last a while, I dropped my head back on the rocker to rest.

The father of one of the babies came into my adjusted field of vision. He, too, sat in a rocking chair, his head back, resting. This is a common sight in our unit, so I can't explain why I looked closer. A young man, late twenties, I'd guess, his face bore lines put there by worry and lost sleep. His child was very ill; the outcome was uncertain.

For just a moment, I saw him through different eyes. And his struggles, his sorrow touched my heart. Tears blurred my vision and threatened to fall, so I excused myself.

This incident shook me. I remembered how hard-hearted the experienced nurses had seemed to me when I was new. When had my heart become hard? I hadn't been aware that I'd raised a barrier until it slipped.

The late Keith Green said during one of his concerts that he worried that his heart was getting hard. He wanted God to change him, to make his heart like baby skin. Jesus' heart must be like that. Jesus was often moved with compassion. He wept for his friends and for Jerusalem. He is "touched with the feeling of our infirmities" (Heb. 4:15 KJV).

Walking around in this profession with a soft heart won't be easy. But I want to be like Jesus. I want his heart in me, not this hard, crusty one.

God, your God, will cut away the thick calluses on
your heart … freeing you to love God, your God,
with your whole heart and soul and live, really live.
—Deuteronomy 30:6 MSG

Day 34: Clean

O great chief, light a candle in my heart,
that I may see what is in it,
and sweep the rubbish from your dwelling place.[11]
—African schoolgirl's prayer

I KNOW HOW TO scrub a wound. I learned it in the ER. I was a mother before I became an RN, and my children noticed the difference in technique and complained—loudly.

The difference? Before I was a nurse, I gently ran water over the scrape, gingerly applied a little soap or peroxide, and finished up with a bandage and a kiss. After nursing school, I soaped a washcloth, rubbed the abrasion, rinsed, resoaped; then scrubbed some more. I made it my mission to get all the dirt out. I still finished with a kiss, but only when the wound was as clean as I could get it. And their wounds healed. No infections. No festering. No antibiotics.

If only I could scrub my heart that clean. It can be a dirty place, but it's hard to reach. Sometimes the dirt is obvious: a lie told, a confidence broken, a rumor spread. Other times, I'm unaware of the mess or have hidden it very well: jealousy, dislike, or pride. I may sense that something is wrong in there or I may never give it a thought. God's Word says, "The heart is hopelessly dark and deceitful, a puzzle that no one can figure out. But I, God, search the heart and examine the mind. I get to the heart of the human. I get to the root of things. I treat them as they really are, not as they pretend to be" (Jer. 17:9–10 MSG).

Like an undiagnosed infection, hidden sin spreads. David, a man who knew about both sin and God, tells us to examine ourselves and, more importantly, open our hearts to God's inspection. The process won't be painless, but the results will be well worth the pain.

Search me, O God, and know my heart:
try me, and know my thoughts:
And see if there be any wicked way in me,
and lead me in the way everlasting.
—Psalm 139:23–24 KJV

Day 35: Buck Up

CATHERINE WORKS BESIDE ME in the NICU. We've survived many a hideous shift, in part, I think, because of something she says. When things are at their very worst, Catherine will look me in the eye and say, "Buck up. We've just got to buck up and do this."

She's right.

We do.

In 2 Chronicles 20, the Israelites were about to be invaded by a great force. The country of Judah united and prayed for God's help. They admitted that they didn't know what to do, and they looked to God. A man named Jahaziel, moved by God, prophesied, saying, "This is God's war, not yours.... You won't have to lift a hand in this battle; just stand firm ... and watch God's saving work for you take shape. Don't be afraid, don't waver. March out boldly tomorrow—God is with you" (vv. 15–17 MSG).

Now, even though the battle was God's, the people still had a responsibility. They had to show up. They had to stand firm and be unafraid. They had to "gird up their loins" (buck up?) and go where the battle was. (Even if you don't remember this story, you can guess that God won this battle. In their confusion, the enemies of Judah ended up killing each other.)

Our struggles can overwhelm us. We may feel inadequate. We may *be* inadequate—we're human, aren't we? None of that matters.

We have a God who cares about us in the midst of our troubles. When we feel powerless and don't know what to do, we can pray.

And then, buck up.

God said this once and for all;
how many times have I heard it repeated?
"Strength comes straight from God."
—Psalm 62:11 MSG

Day 36: Caring

SOMETIMES I CATCH MYSELF not liking people. I tell myself it's okay; it's normal to dislike an annoying or demanding or needy person. I make excuses for myself because I hear the conversations in the break room: the other nurses feel the same as I do about this family or that. I tell myself I treat everyone alike. I smile, ask the right questions, and listen to the answers. I go out of my way to take care of their problems.

But I don't like them. It's a problem.

Most of us know when we're unloved. Maybe body language gives it away; maybe subtler cues. I'm probably not fooling anyone.

The Bible says, "If I speak in the tongues of men and of angels, but have not love, I am only a resounding gong or a clanging cymbal" (1 Cor. 13:1). God wants us to follow the way of love. It's cheating to say, "I love them—I just don't like them."

Somehow I can't picture Jesus treating people the way I do—listening with half an ear, tolerating their presence rather than enjoying it. He'd be tuned in and loving them.

Caring.

So where does that leave me? Can I manufacture a feeling I don't have?

I don't know, but God wouldn't ask me to do the impossible—but wait! God asked people to do that all through the Bible. The answer, as always, is in the Book.

Love is produced in our lives, like fruit, when we remain in an intimate relationship with Jesus. Fruit doesn't come from effort, but from relationship. (See John 15.) Jesus says to remain in his love, then tells us to "love each another as I have loved you" (John 15:12). How? "God has poured out his love into our hearts by the Holy Spirit, whom he has given us" (Rom. 5:5).

What he asks of us, he also provides.

**May the Lord make your love increase and
overflow for each other and for everyone else.**
—1 Thessalonians 3:12

Day 37: A Time to Cry

I AM A CRIER. My daughter says this is genetic as she is also afflicted. It gets in the way of my work at times. I need a clear head to get through my shift without hurting anyone, so I asked God to help me not to cry at work. Because repressing the sadness indefinitely would be unhealthy, I use my car on the drive home as a place to lament. (I wait until I get home if I think I'm really going to lose it.)

Here, in glassed-in solitude, I weep. Sometimes, I yell at God—and I haven't been struck dead yet.

Instead, sometimes I feel as if Jesus is in the empty passenger seat, grieving with me. When I pull into the driveway, I know God has heard me. I know that I lack heaven's perspective. I can't understand what God is up to. But God cares, and he is not diminished or angry when I am brutally honest with him.

Christian friends have told me that they feel pressured to put on a happy face for the world, as if to reinforce the idea that Christianity solves all of their earthly problems. This false face, this perkiness, may actually chase people away from following Jesus. After all, who needs another mask to wear?

The Old Testament is full of crying and complaints. One entire book, Lamentations, mourns over the Babylonian exile. Many of David's songs are laments, crying out to God in sorrow. Could it be that God expects us to bring our distress to him—to lay it all out before him? Like we would do with a friend?

Jesus is a friend like that, "a man of sorrows and acquainted with grief" (Isa. 53:3 NASB). When your heart is broken, he's right there.

Surely our griefs He Himself bore,
And our sorrows He carried.

—Isaiah 53:4 NASB

Day 38: I Can't Do This Anymore!

DON'T YOU JUST FEEL like quitting sometimes? All jobs have their aggravations, but nursing wears a big bull's-eye on its back, attracting the darts of frustration.

Nurses have tons of responsibility without a matching amount of authority. We've made great strides since our handmaiden days, but our minds are still undervalued. We are the facilitators of the health-care system, and much of what we do is invisible. We schedule tests, coordinate care, spot problems, fix conflicts—and we do it so well that everything appears to be falling into place of its own accord. People notice our work when it goes undone, but it fades into the background otherwise.

Nurses deal with people at their worst. Sick people can be irritable, upset, and sometime downright rude. Even though we understand this and can sympathize, the unpleasantness becomes wearing as the shift goes on. Our colleagues on the health-care team are under a lot of pressure too. Their stress can ramp up the tension to a whole new level.

What do most of us do in response? Grit our teeth? Roll our eyes? Try harder? We may tell ourselves we can still be loving servants of God even if we have to force it.

This is a lie. And a recipe for disaster.

Running on empty isn't the answer. God doesn't want us to be stressed out and uptight—no different from those who don't know Jesus. Jesus prayed for his followers to have the full measure of his joy inside them. (See John 17:13.) When we are happy and loving, we draw others to Jesus.

When we're empty, he'll fill us if we let him. If we don't, we'll have nothing to offer anyone else.

The joy of the LORD *is* our strength (Neh. 8:10 KJV).

Though you have not seen him, you love him;
and even though you do not see him now,
you believe in him and are filled with
an inexpressible and glorious joy.

—1 Peter 1:8

Day 39: Lesson from a Code

LAST NIGHT I TOOK part in a code. I've been thinking about it ever since. We performed well as a team but we didn't know why the patient was dying. So we proceeded stepwise through the process, covering all the bases. No response. Just when we were about to give up, our final, last-ditch bold effort saved the patient's life.

The problem? Cardiac tamponade.

Fluid had accumulated in the sac around the heart. When the heart became smaller during systole, the fluid filled the sac so the heart couldn't expand during diastole. In effect, it emptied itself by contracting, then could not refill. Electrical signals continued. The heart muscle struggled on until a doctor placed a needle through the chest into the pericardial sac and drew off the problematic fluid.

In the aftermath, I am struck by how I sometimes find

myself in a similar state spiritually. I let other things crowd in around my heart, Christ's home. I spend myself in futile efforts and find myself incapable of resting so I can be refilled. I feel as though Jesus is talking to me as well as to Martha when he gently scolds her about being "worried and bothered about so many things; but only one thing is necessary" and says that her sister Mary had chosen that good thing—to sit at his feet (Luke 10:41–42 NASB).

In last night's code, one action saved a life. No other action would have sufficed. When the physician removed what didn't belong—leaving the one thing that did—life overcame death.

Great Physician, I give up. Take away the things that trouble my heart so that you, my one thing, can fill it. In Jesus' name I pray. Amen.

**Do not let your hearts be troubled
and do not be afraid.**
—John 14:27

Day 40: His Hands

OUR HANDS ARE A bridge to the patient. Watch your coworkers' hands (or your own) and see. Nurses draw up medications, straighten linens, and write in charts. We pat shoulders, insert IVs, and support unsteady steps. Oh, sure we use our minds. Our hearts are involved. But our hands are the point of contact with the patient. On a good day, we have the satisfaction of massaging a weary back, our hands fully caught up in caring. We make a difference for that person at that moment.

Even so, our hands aren't pretty. They're chapped from frequent hand washing. Our nails are bare to prevent infection. Our unadorned hands will never grace the pages of the fashion magazines. But when you look more deeply, you start to see. Skills, long-used to the point of habit, have granted dexterity and eloquence to these plain hands. As in the hands of a pianist, the beauty of the work is embedded in muscle and bone.

Jesus, too, worked with his hands. He measured and sawed, pounded and smoothed the furniture he made. He reached out to children, laying his hands on them as he prayed. He grasped the hand of a young girl and brought her back to life. He touched blind eyes to make them see. He tore the bread and poured the wine. He opened his fists to receive the nails.

Jesus loved with his hands.

Now—in a much smaller way—so do we.

And Jesus, moved with compassion, put forth his hand, and touched him.
—Mark 1:41 KJV

Notes

1. "Nurses Cannot Be too Posh to Wash," BBC News. May 10, 2004. News.bbc.co.uk/hi/health/3701855.stm. Accessed May 8, 2005.

2. Alexander, J., *Nursing* magazine advertisement (date unknown).

3. Maxfield, D., J. Grenny, R. McMillan, K. Patterson, and A. Switzler, "Silence Kills: The Seven Crucial Conversations for Healthcare," *AACN & VitalSmarts*, L.C. www.aacn.org/aacn/pubpolcy.hsf/files/SilenceKillsExecSum/$file/SilenceKillsExecSum.pdf. Accessed May 8, 2005.

4. Mother Teresa, "Reflections from Mother Teresa of Calcutta," *Missionaries of the Blessed Sacrament.* www.acfp2000.com/Sections/sec8.htm. Accessed May 10, 2005.

5. "Nurses are 'Most Trusted'—Again," *Nursing* 2005, 35, no. 3 (March, 2005): 35.

6. Rogers, A., W. Hwant, L. Scott, L. Aiken, and D. Dinges, "The Working Hours of Hospital Staff Nurses and Patient Safety," *Health Affairs.* 2004; 23; 202–212.

7. Peterson, Andrew, "Steady As She Goes," *Clear to Venus.* Watershed Records, 2001.

8. Parish, Fawn, *It's All About You, Jesus: A Fresh Call to an Undistracted Life.* Reprinted by permission of Thomas Nelson, Inc., Nashville, TN. Copyright © 2001. All rights reserved.

9. Kohn, L., J. Corrigan, M. Donaldson, eds., *To Err is Human: Building a Safer Health System.* Washington, DC: National Academy Press, 2000, 127.

10. *Patient Safety: Preventing Medical Errors.* Orlando Regional Medical Center, Self-Learning Packet, 2004, 7.

11. "African Schoolgirl's Prayer," *2000 Years of Prayer.* Copyright © 1999 by Michael Counsell. Used by permission of Morehouse Publishing.

*Additional copies of this and other Honor products
are available wherever good books are sold.*

*If you have enjoyed this book,
or if it has had an impact on your life,
we would like to hear from you.*

Please contact us at:

*HONOR BOOKS
Cook Communications Ministries, Dept. 201
4050 Lee Vance View
Colorado Springs, CO 80918
Or visit our Web site:
www.cookministries.com*

HONOR **HB** BOOKS